Xenopho
The Aussies

Ken Hunt

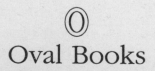

Oval Books

Published by Oval Books
335 Kennington Road
London SE11 4QE

Telephone: (0171) 582 7123
Fax: (0171) 582 1022
E-mail: info@ovalbooks.com

First published by Ravette Publishing.
This edition published by Oval Books.

First edition 1993
Revised 1994
Reprinted 1995, 1997
Updated & revised 1997
Reprinted 1998
New edition 1999

Series Editor – Anne Tauté

Cover designer – Jim Wire, Quantum
Printer – Cox & Wyman Ltd

Contents

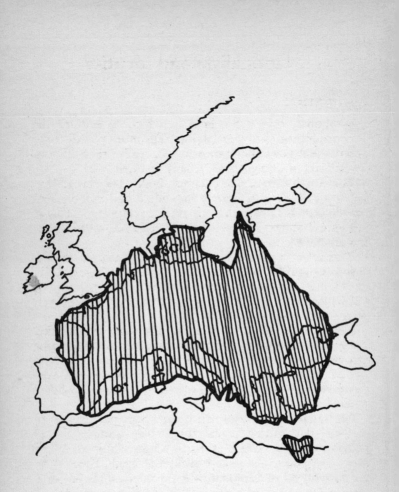

What European background could prepare you for an almost barren landscape with just five living souls per square mile, stretching over an area 56 times greater than England?

Nationalism and Identity

Forewarned

Xenophobes, this is the land in which to indulge the perverse pleasures of your phobia. The more you discover about the Aussies the more you will realize that all your worst fears of foreigners are totally justified.

The Aussies share one common bond, one thread that binds a collection of fiercely individual and independent people together. They are all stark raving mad. This is not entirely surprising: you would need to be a little crazy to actually live there.

If proof of this collective state of insanity is needed, cast your mind back to the last game of Aussie Rules Football you witnessed (hopefully through the security of a television screen). This is the sport the Aussies call their own – with pride.

Never make the error of underestimating the Aussies. They love to portray a casual disregard for everything around them, but no-one accidentally achieves a lifestyle as relaxed as theirs. Their character reflects this inconsistency between attitude and lifestyle – nothing is what it seems.

Australians do not go in for an emotional display of national flags and patriotic songs. The groundswell of patriotic fervour which is periodically whipped up by press and politicians is kept well concealed. There is no need to tell other Aussies how great the country is – they already know and who else is there worth convincing?

One almost certain way to embarrass an Aussie is to bring up the subject of the national anthem. Most don't even know the name of it. Nobody but politicians (slime-bags one and all) knows all the words.

In 1984 the Federal Government proclaimed *Advance*

Australia Fair as the national anthem. This was a real blow after everyone had spent so much time and effort at school trying to master *God Save the Queen*.

Try not to laugh at official functions when an awful mumbling sound commences at the same time as the tune of the national anthem. This allows the Aussies to gain time while they sort out which song it is. By the time it reaches the first chorus most people are brave enough to venture a few words; between choruses it's back to dumb mumbling.

At unofficial occasions, if the national anthem is called for, everyone will burst into a confused* rendering of *Waltzing Matilda*. After all, no bloody politician is going to tell an Aussie what song to sing.

Special Relationships

Ever since Britain started dumping her undesirables in Australia, she has been seen in a parental light.

The first European arrivals wore clothing emblazoned with POHMIE (Prisoners of His Majesty in Exile). The fact that the English are still called 'Pommies' today is not to be taken as an insult. Well, it is an insult but an Aussie will only insult a friend – so it's not really an insult.

Today Britain is seen a bit like a mother who kicked her child out of the nest. After 200 years of direct and indirect mothering Australia was growing well. But it was not yet self-sufficient. It enjoyed a preferred trading

*This is because they are still unsure. Even the title is uncertain. *Waltzing* means to keep walking (dodging the vagrancy laws); *Matilda/My Tilda/M'tilda* is the pole slung over the shoulder carrying all your worldly possessions in a cloth bundle.

partner status with Mother which was a great help in competing against bigger kids.

The European Community was the cuckoo.

Since this financial break with the UK, the Aussies are battling to support the lifestyle they had become used to while they were in the nest. But does any of this worry them? Do they hold any animosity towards the Brits? None at all. These things were all done by politicians and every Aussie knows that politicians have no connection with real people and real issues.

Britain is no longer considered important. It's a tiny island, crowded with people, 13,000 miles away. The best use it serves is to give the cricketers a bit of exercise now and again. It's not a bad spot either for entertainers to get extra exposure on their way to better things.

The other nation that rates a special mention in terms of relationships is the Kiwis, but only because, being so close, Aussies can't ignore them as much as they would like.

How They See Themselves

In the 1950s and 60s the English media carried advertisements promoting immigration to Australia. The typical Aussie man was portrayed as young, big, bronzed and spending all day at the beach. The Aussie woman was young, shapely, bronzed and also spent all day at the beach.

These advertisements lured many unsuspecting Poms to their doom. For their ten quid fare they had to endure at least two years down under. During these two years many lost the will to return to England.

In the 1980s, Australian television carried an updated image of the bronze male hero. His name was Norm. He

7

was 30-40 years old and had a huge pot belly. He sat in front of the television watching sport all day. Beer in hand, of course. Nowadays they seem to have lost interest in an image. They don't care what people think.

The Aussies were happy to have their trials of life portrayed as glamorous. Their attitude was that any Poms stupid enough to fall for such garbage deserved to live in Australia. Compassion has never been a strong point.

That their country is seen as sports orientated is amusing to most Aussies. The percentage who actually watch sport is very low. The silent majority and the apathetic middle really only become enthusiastic about sport when an Aussie team looks likely to beat another, larger, nation.

Aussies, if you set aside the vocal minority, see themselves as international underdogs. It is a good position to be in. There is no shame in losing since no other country can rightfully expect much of them; nor is there much to be gained in beating them (being a smaller foe). Both of these views are very useful; neither presents any serious demand for an Australian victory.

How They Would Like Others to See Them

To suggest to an Aussie that they come from the breeding stock of criminals is personal lunacy. They would be quick to point out that that stock was imported mainly from England. Further, they regret to this day that they couldn't afford the criminal class of a better country.

In any case, in the 70 or so years of transportation, only 160,000 convicts arrived. It's a drop in the ocean compared with the number of free immigrants.

The fact that the present citizenry largely grew from deportees and fortune hunters (the quick-buck gold seekers of the 19th century) is not entirely lost on the population. It's all too obvious in constant exposures of political corruption and ineptitude.

But Aussies would like to replace the outworn image of their beloved country being a convict settlement. They're not crooks, they're people with initiative. They would like others to see them as rightful world leaders in independent thinking.

How They See Others

Aussies have had a crash course in the 20th century in coming to terms with other nationalities.

Australia is now home to a mixed bag of 18 million people – less than 1% of whom are descendants of its original indigenous people.

Almost any nationality you can name is represented there – the British, Irish, Italians, Greeks, Slavs, Dutch, Germans, Spanish, Poles, Vietnamese, Indians, Lebanese, Turks, Chinese – and all have taught the Aussies their own brand of rudimentary international relations.

The media recognize this cosmopolitan influence and ignore it. Page four of the newspaper will have the token item of international news. Television news usually has a few items of overseas stuff – doom and gloom coverage just sufficient to remind people that there is a world outside Australia and to reaffirm their belief that this is the only place to live.

But you have to sympathize with this lack of interest in international affairs: it's all so far away. If a country does not play cricket, rugby, hockey, golf, tennis or compete in the Olympics – it doesn't exist. Even some of the countries competing in the Olympic Games come as a complete surprise.

Character

Lurking inside every Aussie is the greatest complexity of characters imaginable. Portrayed as a single intelligence no logic is visible, but if viewed in the light of component traits some of the fog may lift.

The Aussie Battler

Large tracts of farming land were opened up under Government land settlement schemes. These schemes were all roughly the same: take one naïve family, add one axe, twenty sheets of corrugated iron, one packet of seed, sprinkle with empty promises, then dump in the middle of the bush.

Life for the early settlers was a constant battle. They battled against the heat, they battled against the bureaucracy, the lack of water, the flies, the snakes, the weather and the isolation. It was a hard and lonely existence. It gave life to a special and hardy breed of people. Mick (Crocodile) Dundee is one of them. Mick and a handful of his friends still exist. They are alive and well on farms, in the wheatbelt and on stations*.

Aussies are happy to bask in the reflected glory of the early settlers. They harbour romantic aspirations towards adversity and deprivation. But today the vast majority live in the cities and cling to the coastal fringes. Their biggest battle is to keep the leaves out of the pool.

The one isolation that is still shared by all is the isolation from the culture of Europe. This is not considered a hardship.

---

*Station is a term originally used by the Colonial Government for their own agricultural and pastoral establishments where convicts were 'stationed'.

The Underdog Syndrome

The Aussies love the underdog: the little bloke who tries hard, who challenges the champion or the inflexible establishment. This underpins their continuous challenge of authority and of the status quo.

The athlete striving to get to the top of a sport can expect total admiration and support. This is the true champion – the people's champion, and fighter of a cause. The reigning champion is nothing more than a goal post: something for the people's champion to focus on. This can be a bit demoralizing for the reigning champion who only yesterday was the people's champion.

Every Aussie knows full well that all champions are conceited and therefore deserve to be knocked off their pedestal. This is the 'tall poppy' syndrome: stand out from the crowd and you'll be cut down to size. Trying to grow tall is admirable. Actually succeeding is inexcusable.

Open a business alongside a successful one and look poor, inefficient and as though you are struggling. It's a guaranteed way to snare all your neighbour's customers.

Xenophobes should not miss a golden opportunity: this characteristic can be used to good effect. If you want to enjoy being disliked, all you have to do is appear popular, happy and friendly. Every Aussie knows full well that no-one is as nice as they seem. You are therefore immediately subjected to suspicion and contempt.

If you prefer to be liked, all you have to do is act brash, sullen and self-reliant. Every Aussie knows full well that no-one is as bad as they seem. If you happen to have some unfortunate traits then you, more than anyone else, need friends.

Just how much development in Australia has been stifled by this perplexing syndrome it is impossible to estimate. However, with very obvious support for trying rather than succeeding, there is clearly more personal satisfaction in remaining the underdog.

Irreverence

You will not shut an Aussie up. Nor can you stop them from doing something they have already decided to do. There is simply no threat you can hold over them, they answer only to their own principles.

Such primitive moral foundations could do nothing but produce the most irreverent country of people imaginable. In the New South Wales Parliament during a passionate debate a politician described another member of the House as "not having the brains of a donkey". (This would certainly not be regarded as particularly perceptive by the electorate, nor a particular disadvantage for a politician. It is the norm.)

The Speaker demanded a retraction and much to his surprise got it immediately. The offender sprang to his feet: "Mister Speaker, I was wrong and I apologize. The Honourable Member *does* have the brains of a donkey."

Insults are almost terms of endearment and if you don't have a nickname it can only be because of some severe personality disorder.

If you had a leg amputated your nickname would probably be 'stumpy'. A religious zealot would be called 'god', and one of those born-again evangelical church groups would be referred to as the 'clap and jumps'.

Nothing is sacrosanct. An Aussie introduced his frail 80-year-old mother, who had only 10% vision, with the remark: "This is me mum, she don't look too good."

When Lindy Chamberlain was accused of the murder of her baby a huge controversy ensued. The Chamberlains claimed that a dingo had stolen the child from their

Ayers Rock camp site. Within days there were T-shirts being sold with the message 'The dingo is innocent'.

Behaviour

If you mistakenly expect to encounter 'normal' behaviour in Australia, consider the environment in which these people live.

The country's location is not normal. This is not a cheap crack about it hanging upside down. This refers to the racial origin of the majority of the population. Practically everybody is living out of their traditional climatic zone.

The trees are not normal. They don't drop leaves – they drop bark. Many of the species of gum (eucalyptus) trees shed great sheets of bark. They are all evergreens. You will find more bark under the trees than fallen leaves.

The two ambassadorial birds are not normal. The emu, included on the coat of arms, doesn't fly. The kookaburra doesn't sing – it laughs. Another thing about this exalted kookaburra – it's a raptor: its staple diet is smaller birds.

The rivers aren't normal. A standard joke in Victoria is that their biggest river flows upside down. They mean the Murray which has more mud in the surface water than it has on the river bed.

Against this background no serious-minded person could possibly expect normal behaviour from the human inhabitants. This is the country that thinks of bungee jumping as a normal weekend activity.

The Aussies do not wave like any other nationality. The movement they call their 'salute' is a constant hand wave in front of the face. Quite by chance this keeps the flies off their faces. You will notice the old bushies' salute is much slower than the townies'. This is experience, not laziness. You only want the flies off your face. They aren't heavy, therefore those sitting on your back are no problem. If you wave too fast you will disturb these as well and so keep the whole lot in the air.

Even the lack of a solution is a solution to them. In Queensland when Castlemaine were having trouble spelling the proposed name of their beer they used XXXX instead. (It was alleged by the other states who used to compete vigorously with their own brands – Swan in the West, Tooheys in New South Wales, VB in Victoria – that the word they were looking for was 'CRAP'.)

There is nothing normal about the behaviour of the Aussies. This is a country where eccentric behaviour, providing it is well done, is considered a great personal attribute. Any form of eccentricity will do.

The Family

One way in which the Aussie family behaves markedly differently from their European ancestors shows when you look at their extended family groups, or rather, their lack of an extended family.

In the past 40 years the population has rocketed to more than double its strength. As keen as they are on procreation, much of this growth has actually come from immigration. There's nothing like having the rest of your family on the other side of the world to break the ties.

The Aussies are also a mobile mob and will live wherever they can get work. This is easily seen in the creation of huge mining communities in remote areas of the country. Even if mum and dad did move near their family, the family would be up and gone again in a few years.

In any case, very few oldies would want to live with their kids. They probably couldn't wait for them to leave home in the first place. And there is no fun in being a live-in babysitter.

Each suburb takes on its own identity. One suburb will have all young families and another may have all retired people. It is therefore unlikely that you would find many suburbs which satisfy the interests of both.

Social Security payments are sufficient to remove any financial dependency and so add to the independence of families. Creation of all forms of independence is instinctive to an Aussie.

Manners

The Aussies have inherited most of their manners and etiquette from the English. This is one of the few areas where tradition is followed. The Aussies have all the same hang-ups.

Men will open doors for women. Hosts will open doors for guests. Bosses will open doors for subordinates. Anyone handy will open doors for someone with a mob of ankle biters (kids, not dogs). And everyone will take the time to smile and say "ta". "Excuse me" scrapes in from time to time, but "Excuse me please" could be pushing it.

The Aussies will always wait their turn for service although queuing is not such a common occurrence. If the place is busy they will prefer to come back later. But if queue you must, why not make the most of it. Conversations between complete strangers are commonplace: it can be a shame to reach the counter sometimes.

Etiquette

Forks on the left, knives on the right and bread, sliced, on your own side plate. Simple.

The great Aussie barbecue does exist and though they don't happen nearly as often as the soap operas would have you believe, you should be prepared for this possibility.

At an outdoor barbecue manners have to be modified. It is considered acceptable to wave your hands around. In fact it's downright essential if you want to keep the flies off your food. If you can't be bothered waving, no worries – the flies don't eat much.

The Aussies mean what they say. If they put a heap of food on the table and say help yourself, that is exactly what they mean. If you meekly sit back and wait to be encouraged further you are going to leave the table hungry.

Picking food up with your hands is acceptable – one hand if you favour the English – two hands if you favour the Americans. But wiping your hands on the curtains is not polite.

If you're invited to a family home for an evening meal you would normally take along a few beers or a bottle of wine. In fact many 'invites' will specify BYOG (Bring Your Own Grog). This could be implied subtlety, by Australian standards. What they really mean is 'kick on the door about seven'.

Greetings

Of all that you see on television there is one bit that is not exaggerated. Aussies do say "G'day". All levels of friendship, all levels of formality and all levels of family familiarity. The first word between two lovers in the morning – "G'day".

The other main greeting would have to be "G'day mate". "G'day Sheila" is a figment of the movie industry's imagination.

The reason why this brief greeting has such universal acceptance is simple, it's the flies. The longer your mouth is open the more flies that can crawl in. The lip movement on the word "G'day" is sudden and only a token. The sound is emitted via the nose.

Social Graces

You may have been led to believe that Aussies are not pretentious. This is utter rubbish. It's just that those with visions of self-importance keep it to themselves or share it (cautiously) only with the like-minded.

In one way they consider it extremely poor manners to show any sign that one person is better than another. In another respect they can think it a real laugh that someone can be so far 'up themselves'.

Selection of guests for small gatherings will therefore be all important. If you are pretentious and are doing the inviting, be sure to invite only pretentious people. One slip up and the 'fair dinkum' guest will have great fun at the expense of all the others.

On the other hand, when a pretentious person receives an invite his concern must be that perhaps he is being invited as the unwitting entertainment for the other guests.

Being pretentious is thus the most severe form of social bad manners. If you display such a failing, beware of the Aussie response. It's not enough for them merely to get the dagger in – they like to turn it and turn it.

Bodily Contact

The Aussies are not a very physically demonstrative group. In fact, there are basically only three times when an Aussie would touch another person: at a funeral, during love-making and when handshaking.

A comforting hug at a funeral is heartfelt and is done without inhibition. It is the most unhurried display, public or private, that you are likely to see.

Touching during love-making is unavoidable. However, as the whole process takes only thirty seconds and is always done in private, it is not something worthy of too much attention.

Handshaking is very important. (None of your Eastern European limp-wristed, dead fish type of handshake either. This is a man's country. If you've got muscles, use them; if not, fake it.) Men will never offer their hand to a woman, and any woman so 'liberated' as to offer hers to a man will enjoy the pleasure of seeing an uncomfortable late thrust of his hand towards her.

Sense of Humour

To live in Australia, Aussies have had to develop a strong sense of humour. Besides, it's a cheap form of entertainment and helps pass the time.

Their sardonic and laconic attitude creeps into every conversation. If you display any form of weakness they will tear at it like a dog with a bone.

This irreverent and ruthless lot will aim their jokes at any country and people with any advantage or disadvantage. This is not a back-stabbing population. They will tell anti-English jokes to the English, anti-Irish jokes to the Irish and Ethiopian jokes to anorexics. The English can expect to hear:

Q: How can you tell when the plane that lands is full of Poms?
A: When the motors stop, the whining continues.

The Kiwis (the butt-end of much Aussie humour) are very quickly reminded of the special relationship they have with their sheep by such as:

Q: Why do New Zealand men marry New Zealand women?
A: Because sheep can't cook.

Q: What do you call a New Zealander with 40 sheep?
A: A pimp.

To Parliament for another example. A bill was being debated which affected rural people. One of the elderly rural backbenchers felt so involved as to actually awaken and make an extremely rare address. He started in his slow way:

"Mis—ter Spea—ker, I am a count—ry member."

At this point, before he could say another word, came a cry from the front benches:

"We remember!"

The Aussies can easily laugh at themselves but of course, with their isolation they have often had little choice. But beware, they don't care for outsiders to do it.

Beyond the Black Stump

Stories about the outback* are part of Aussie character and humour. This is the stuff that is a bit like spice – it's not a noticeable proportion of the bulk, but without it the meal just wouldn't be the same.

Ringers, jackaroos and jillaroos are the workers on the outback stations and there is no use trying to think of an English equivalent. Some of these properties are a thousand square miles in size and they breed their own brand of person. Here frustration is a waste of good effort. If something goes wrong they fix it. If it's hot – it's hot. If it's dry and dusty nobody is going to waste time complaining about it.

One of these ringers, with the nickname of Cowboy, was working down south after many years at the very top of the professional rodeo scene. He decided to attend a first aid course and was an instant sensation.

Every time the instructor talked about a particular broken bone and how to ease it, Cowboy described the pain of that type of break. The instructor was not able to come up with a bone that Cowboy had not broken.

Cowboy told a story of a ringer he was working with to repair a large windmill. The ringer was at the top and he was on the ground. The ringer screams out to stop the mill "Me fingers are stuck in the cogs – wind it backwards so I can get them out!" This was not his lucky day, the mill could be stopped but it could not go backwards.

"Well wind it forward slowly" he calls to the ground. After a bit of winding Cowboy calls up to the ringer "Have you lost any fingers?" "Yea" drawls the ringer and starts giving a running commentary "two off – three off – four off…"

---

*The 'outback' identifies isolated and desolate areas; the 'bush' can be anything which is not a city – including the outback.

Beliefs and Values

Heading the list of Aussie values is the unshakable belief in their own individuality.

They know their country is like no other and can sense a certain shock amongst overseas visitors which confirms them in their view that they are different.

From studying statistics on the diversity of racial backgrounds in Australia it would be easy to conclude that you are looking at a cosmopolitan population. Taken as a bunch and treated in terms of origins this is probably true. But, as every Aussie knows full well, statistics are collected by governments, governments are controlled by politicians and politicians are not to be trusted.

This cosmopolitan image disappears when Aussies are viewed individually. Even those born in another country probably have only that one other country to relate to. The majority have little interest in international affairs and travel overseas very rarely.

For native-born Aussies, travelling overseas is something you do if you are twenty years old and in no particular hurry to complete your education. The first preference for overseas travel is the Asian neighbours. Beer, food and accommodation are cheap. There are even a few places with surf – what more could you want? This might be great fun but it provides little exposure to western cultures.

The more resourceful will find their way to Europe spending every last cent they have in getting there. They also reckon that if you are going that far you may as well 'do' all of Europe. It's not that big.

They return with a lopsided view. They will have seen all the train stations and city centres, located all the youth hostels, learned to survive on bread and cheese for weeks on end, and have been through every free museum.

On top of all this most Aussies are travelling in their summer – European winter.

Throw in the physical isolation of Australia and you have very little external challenge to govern their outlook.

Nature is the biggest single influence on the Aussie attitude. And a very harsh and unforgiving influence it is. Reality, totally uncontrollable, is never far outside the suburban limits.

Pompous traditions, laws, and authority can't be seen as too important when at any time physical considerations arise which may override the situation. For example:

- How can a school child in Alice Springs be expected to get to school if last night's flash flood has cut the road?

- Why would anyone wear a coat and tie to work when it's 110° in the water bag?

- How can a surfer turn up for work if the surf is running?

Flexibility in lifestyle and work practices has always been an essential part of being able to adapt. The convict settlement provided an irreverent attitude to start with and nature has guaranteed an innovative population ever since.

Class

This is a very class conscious society. None of this upper-class, middle-class and lower-class stuff, though. Class is based on character. No-one will give a second thought to family pedigree, income, or which school you attended.

It is a brutally honest class system. There is nothing to blame lack of social acceptance on but yourself. On the other hand, social acceptance is without trial or waiting period for anyone with an honest nature.

You are not likely to be addressed as Mr, Mrs or Ms. If someone went to the bother of giving you a first name, why not use it? If this causes you some discomfort it must be because of some hang-up of your own and if you think that's a problem, wait till you discover your nickname.

How you relate to others is everything. How you dress is up to you. This results in a rather casual sartorial standard but there's nothing wrong with that; it is everyone else that wastes their time on senseless formalities.

Wealth and Success

A short European history, penal estate taxes (virtually non-existent now) and high income tax rates, combined with a 'We've got it, so we might as well spent it' attitude, have ensured that there is not much 'family' wealth in Australia.

Wealth is basically restricted to the entrepreneurs. During the 1980s Australia had so many that they were exporting them. There was such financial success at that time that many people were suddenly very wealthy.

Aussies display their wealth in three main ways.

*   If they're just a bit rich, it's a couple of fancy cars. Something sporty, red and German will do nicely.

*   If they are really rich they buy huge houses in exclusive (i.e. only the rich can afford the rates) suburbs.

*   If they are filthy rich they buy a property where they can boast that they spend their weekends. The stages

are: extravagant beach house, a near-city farm – and top of the 'wozza' (heap) – a vineyard.

The suddenly rich entrepreneurs were regarded with mixed emotions. Their spending power made them powerful and this engendered awe. The fact they were successful also meant that they must be dishonest or at the very kindest 'a bit sharp'. They would obviously sell their mother for a dollar. Referring to the famously wealthy like Alan Bond as 'Bondie' both identifies with success, but also cuts them down to size.

The crash of the financial markets in 1987 and the subsequent collapse of many entrepreneurs was seen as nothing more than them getting exactly what they deserved. Western Australia had more than its share of this class and the jokes started immediately. Take one example:

Two young women walking along St George's Terrace happen upon an ugly toad.

"Psst" says the toad, "I'm really an entrepreneur and have been changed into a toad by a magic spell – kiss me and the spell is broken."

Quick as a flash one of the women scoops up the toad and drops it into her handbag.

"You're not going to kiss that slimy thing are you?" says the companion. "Entrepreneurs aren't worth a cent."

"Course not," said the quick one, "but have you any idea how much a talking toad is worth?"

Money is something you have to have. This must be so or the Aussies would have found a way around it long ago. But there is simply no excuse for putting money ahead of the important things in life.

The only truly acceptable way to accumulate money is by winning it. There is a huge national 'lotto' with millions of dollars to be won three times each week.

If you inherit wealth you're lucky. If you accumulate wealth you're a crook, and if you win a fortune you're a national hero.

Pursuit of Pleasure

Being successful is not all that important. Social status is a foreign concept. When it comes to the crunch there is only one thing the Aussies value – having a good time.

This hedonistic society has got it down to a fine art. The leaders in the field are the surfers. These people have one purpose in life. They surf. In between good surf they drink, eat, sleep, love and, if absolutely unavoidable, work.

This is the embodiment of all that the Aussies hold dear. It is also the curse of every Aussie who has ever had to rely on a surfer to get something done. If the surf's up, you don't have a hope.

This paradoxical situation is repeated constantly throughout society. But the general attitude is "It's no problem – she'll be right mate!"

Domestication and the Suburbs

The domesticated Aussie is an awful phenomenon. The very concept is a contradiction in terms.

These sad characters flock willingly into suburbia with the arrival of children. Perversely the only reason for becoming a parent must be that the children provide the social justification for that move.

All Aussies own their own home. Well, more exactly, they have their name on a title deed, along with a bank or building society. A house is not for ever either, they continually buy and sell houses in an upward spiral of value and size.

In a country with so much nonconformity and character, this perverse leaning to suburbia is totally inexplicable. Perhaps it is human retaliation for the natural peculiarities of the country.

Fanning out from every city are miles and miles of suburbs. These wonderful modern wildernesses, with their carefully designed 'individuality', are undeniably the most uninspired places on earth.

Weekend entertainment for the childless and upwardly mobile is touring the display homes. Concealed in every new suburb are the developers' centres where they have a cluster of houses to flaunt their product. Each centre crawls with sales staff eager to help seal your fate in suburbia.

Every family has two cars in front of its house (bungalow). Also a collection of bicycles, trailers, caravans, boats and anything else that satisfied some passing fancy of the occupants.

House interiors get only cursory attention. The real emphasis is on the exterior. The patio, barbecue, garden and a pool if you can afford the extra loan, are a family's proof of existence.

It is no coincidence that most invites to a family house for dinner are timed so that there is still enough daylight for a proud tour of the latest creation in the yard. This month's treat may be a lopsided brick barbecue, an uneven square of brick paving or a new garden bed.

During the week both parents work to pay off the

loans. The children spend all day at school and return home to maraud around their neighbourhood until dragged inside by the lure of some soap opera.

Emotional release arrives on Saturday between the weekly shopping trip and washing the cars. The kids play sport (whether they want to or not). This is something which involves the whole family. Adults will let off steam by exhorting their kids to 'kill' the opposition. These sideline antics are the closest the suburban Aussie will come to actual participation.

Junior sport gives Dad a great chance to relate to his children. Until this stage in his life, work has seemed more important. He will now spend the whole of the next week dissecting every move they made and should have made. After all he is a well-educated sports spectator.

Sunday morning is 'change the garden around' time. This entails a trip to both the plant nursery and the DIY centre. These huge centres are the true heart of suburban life. One of their principal attractions is that they ensure little time for actual work in the yard.

Today's modern suburbanites favour native plants for their yards. The glorious lawns with colourful shrubs and flowers are making way for designer bush. These Aussies do not see the absurdity of living in such a contrived environment and yet pretending an affinity for their natural bush. Sunday afternoon there is sport on television.

Suburban living is the blight on the Australian character.

Obsessions

Water

There is one obsession so fundamental to Aussies they would never recognize it. They are obsessed with water. Can you blame them? Everybody lives on the coast, on a river or near a lake.

By the way, a 'billabong' is an ox-bow lake, something the movie producers seem happy to overlook in their quest to squeeze the word in as often as they can. The only time you will actually hear the word billabong used is in movies produced for the export market and in the song *Waltzing Matilda*.

If you live alongside the ocean you still need a swimming pool. The logic here is simple; if you live on the water's edge then you, more than anyone, can afford a swimming pool.

Beer Drinking

Nobody could deny beer drinking is the second most obvious obsession. This is certainly undertaken by all Aussies but it is the men who have developed it to cult status. Ask an Aussie if he has a drink problem and his reply will be "Drink problem? We haven't run out, have we?"

Public bars are still very much a man's domain. Women are welcomed but must 'act like men'. Bars, particularly the most macho ones, can present all manner of risks for the unwary xenophobe. A simple insult would be to take your change off the bar while you are still standing there drinking – a blatant display of distrust of those near you. Putting your glass upside down on the bar would be interpreted as an invitation to 'take on' (fight) any person in the pub.

If you are planning to take a few beers around to someone's house, a casual "Whaddaya drink?" would be considered very polite. If you want to drink wine, particularly white wine, you had best do it in the privacy of your own home. The predominant view is that only women and the weak wristed drink white wine. This folklore, however, is not supported by the facts: around three out of every four bottles of wine sold are white.

Beer is always drunk cold. The colder the better. Their obsession with keeping beer cold explains why Aussies drink out of such small glasses – to stop it getting too hot while being held. 'Tinnies' and 'stubbies' are kept in polystyrene coolers. A cool box is called an 'esky' (a brand name, but commonly used, like Kleenex). The size is expressed in terms of the amount of beer it can hold. No self-respecting Aussie would go fishing without at least a two-carton (48 stubby) esky.

Beer bellies are things of great pride. On the Gold Coast (in Queensland – where else?) the annual beer belly contest is the biggest display of male flesh you will ever see. All the ageing Norms of the region waddle proudly on to the podium. For several years, the deputy premier of the State Government was a popular and competitive entrant.

Road Deaths

The Aussies have a perverse obsession with their road toll. The number of dead are reported regularly and in great depth through the media.

With sports commentator-type presentation they will report the yearly road deaths for the state and compare that figure with the previous year. They will give the same detail for the national figures. Occasionally they will compare relative performances between the states, delivered with almost competitive relish.

There are also the motorists and pedestrians who are magically drawn towards vehicles driven by people who have 'just had a couple of beers'. Any link between road deaths and the obsession with drinking is purely coincidental.

Aussies will twist any statistics to their own ends. One statistic doing the rounds was that 40% of drivers in accidents had been drinking. Since this left 60% of drivers who hadn't had a drop, but who still had accidents, it must obviously be safer to drink and drive.

Television

This is essential household entertainment for a country of spectators.

Few Aussies admit to being television addicts, but this is contradicted by the presence of an average of two sets owned per home.

There is only one government-owned channel, the Australian Broadcasting Commission, and this is available in every region – with local input. There is also a wide range of uniformly atrocious commercial channels. Advertisements on these channels run for up to twelve minutes per hour with breaks less than ten minutes apart.

Television news, in the American style, is heavily biased towards the sensational. A few minutes are allocated to international and political matters and the remainder is taken up with advertisements and reports of violence, social injustices and personal tragedies.

You will have no luck in following any of your favourite soap operas in Australia. The Aussie ones are many episodes ahead and any English 'soapies' that are shown are many episodes behind.

In a climate so suited to an outdoor lifestyle this penchant for watching television defies logic.

There are many things about Aussies that defy logic.

Leisure and Pleasure

The most common leisure activity by far is watching the television and all the most enjoyable activities can be done in front of it:

- Sex must top the enjoyable list – this can be done during the advertisements.

- Drinking is second on the list – this can be done between the advertisements and during sex.

- Watching sport is next – this, happily, is actually on the television.

Talking about sex, drinking and sport takes up all the minor spaces and this is done in front of the television, at any time sport is not being shown.

Gambling

It is hardly amazing that in a country full of risk takers, gambling is a major money spinner. Each State has at least one casino. These are universally derided in public but supported in private. The State Governments own the TAB (Totaliser Agency Board) which has a monopoly on (legal) off-course horse betting. They are ably assisted by the Federal Government which uses its radio station to ensure that horse racing is never far from the punter's attention.

In New South Wales sporting and other community organizations can legally operate one-armed bandits in their club rooms. The Aussies flock to these clubs in droves. Part of the profits from the gambling goes towards keeping the cost of meals low and providing popular live entertainment.

The clubs are so profitable that even after the state government has taken its share there is still an embarrassing amount left. This leftover must be spent on members' facilities or on the aims of the association.

It has meant some massive extravagances for the members. A small-time football club could have luxury holiday villas available free of charge for every one of the players.

The greed of the clubs in separating people from as much money as possible is only matched by the rush of people to give it to them. In the north of the state they send buses into Queensland to snare car-less people who might otherwise be denied their opportunity to contribute. Losses are seen not so much as a waste, but more as a magnanimous gesture to the needy.

The lure of the clubs is obvious. It's not the cheap tucker and entertainment – it's the Aussies' passion to have a go at beating the system.

Annual Holiday

Once a year, whether they want to or not, the family take a holiday. This is an horrific experience that is enjoyed by nobody.

The first decision is which beach to get close to with

the tent (Aussie tents are massive things) or caravan. After much argument they always end up going back to the same spot as they have been to every other year.

Summer in Australia means hot days. Try and imagine a family crammed in a car along with the dog, fishing gear, food, cooking equipment, boogie boards (small surf boards), bicycles and a couple of eskies. This car is travelling in the sun, in a line of traffic and for many hours. Summer holidays don't stand a hope of success.

Once settled at the beach, with the kids 'somewhere', the parents slip straight into serious drinking and 'gum bashing' with the equally frustrated neighbours. It's a kind of self-help fraternity.

Each evening the surprise that no travel guide ever tells you about arrives – the mossies. If you are lucky, by this time you will have had such a skinful of booze that you won't feel the little blood suckers. Everyone else has to coat themselves with the Aeroguard – the malodorous insect repellent spray known to cool even the strongest of ardours.

After two weeks of blazing sun, sand in the food, mossie bites, flies on everything, spiders in the tent, a snake scare and busted marriage, limbs and equipment, comes the long hot miserable drive home (to the television, air conditioning and swimming pool).

Other Holidays

The Aussies get a generous number of paid holidays. Normal annual leave is four weeks per year and people on shift work or in isolated areas will get more. While on holiday they get 17½% loading on top of their normal pay – presumably to compensate for the extra beer they need to drink to cope with the ordeal.

They also get ten paid public holidays and at least seven of these result in long weekends.

The big Aussie holiday surprise is 'long service leave'. This is 13 weeks' paid holiday every 10, 15 or 20 years depending on the particular award. Long service leave has its roots in Australia's European background. So many people demanded extended holidays at some time in their working life for a sojourn to their former homeland that it became structured in the pay schemes.

Eating and Drinking

No shocks await you at meal times. For all the wide origins of the population, it's English culture which has formed the structure of meals and eating times.

The weather also has a bit to do with it. It is only in the last 30 years that the population finally realized how insane it was to have a hot roast meal for Sunday lunch all through the summer. Christmas lunches were a nightmare.

Working hours are basically 8 to 5 with an hour for lunch. This clearly defines the eating times. In the tropics and in summer dinner would be quite late – to let the worst of the heat wear off.

For the tourist trade there have been recent trends towards cooking the indigenous animals. But for the old-timers particularly, kangaroo is definitely a last resort. For one thing it smells like hell as it cooks.

One surprise is the almost total lack of rabbit meat sold. The country is infested with them. They were introduced by the English to provide Sunday shooting exercise (as were foxes).

During the Great Depression these wild rabbits provided a valuable source of meat. The usual description, to deceive the kids, was 'underground mutton'.

With 130 million sheep in the country, this is obviously the largest source of meat. The meat of sheep is divided into three categories – by their teeth: lamb – anything up to a two-tooth; hoggett – from two- to four-tooth; and mutton – from six-tooth right up to a broken-mouth ewe.

The Meat Pie

The national food dish would have to be the meat pie. This is revolting. It is eaten hot and, in ideal circumstances, standing up and surrounded by flies.

In Queensland you would eat them with a mushy green pea gunge on top. In South Australia you would have them floating in a mushy green pea gunge. In most other places you flood them with tomato ketchup to disguise the taste.

In Queensland, particularly in the industrial estates, you can buy these pies from 'pie-ologists'. These are a cult of vendors who have an oven on their utility and sell hot pies from dusty bays on the side of the road. You can usually see the cloud of flies before you see the oven.

The wave of dust following the arrival of each car puts a wonderful crust on the pies. But the real attraction of these vendors is their advertising claims:

'Bill's pies – the best in town.
50 million blowflies can't be wrong.'

The flood of American fast food outlets is carving huge roads into this market. But at the end of the day, men eat pies.

The Off Licence

It should be no surprise that the only form of mainstream retailing to differ significantly from England is the off-licence, or liquor store, or bottle shop, or grog shop. Bearing in mind that this is both a car culture and a drinking culture, what could be more natural than a drive-in liquor store. Normally these are huge affairs with an option for service to the car (very useful if you're already 'full as a goog') or to get out and wander around.

Aussie wines are no longer a secret. The good news is that the best wines aren't exported. A wine shop without any 'froggy' wines on the shelves presents a bewildering range of Aussie brands and varieties you will never have heard of. Even in the wine-producing districts the liquor stores will carry wines from all other regions.

Beer is often not displayed in the quantities you might expect. Normal refrigerated displays simply cannot cope with the Aussie thirst for cold beer by the carton. It's a matter of going into the coolroom and getting your own supplies.

Another difference is the emphasis on sweets, potato chips (crisps) and soft drinks. After all, in this age of family sensitivity, no self-respecting Aussie male could pick up 30 dollars' worth of booze for himself without a soft drink for the kids and a bar of chocolate for the wife.

Health and Hygiene

If you have good health you have nothing to worry about. If you have poor health – well that's the way it goes sometimes. So why start worrying now?

The Aussies are plagued by government programmes to promote better diet and reduce smoking. But what would the government know? While there has been a measurable decrease in smoking this is due more to the fact there is hardly anywhere left that you can do it.

Besides, it would be a clear disservice to the doctors if this 'health thing' was to catch on. Doctors have a living to make too, you know.

Aussie doctors are fabulous. They are practically free, and easy to get to see. Hospital waiting lists are insignificant and the hospitals are friendly, efficient and spotlessly clean. What more can be said? Get sick there and you're in luck.

The Flying Doctor

This unique Aussie answer to the medical problems of isolated areas is one of Australia's most proudly held public services. It is largely funded by voluntary contributions from the public, and support is as strong in the cities as it is in the country areas.

This is a crucial service to the inland stations, mining towns, aboriginal communities, weather stations and all the other places people are crazy enough to choose.

The less visible side of the service is the radio network which has been created to enable it to operate.

Aussies in remote areas use the radio system for schooling (School of the Air), neighbourly gossip and business, district weather warnings and all the other things that those with telephones and ready transport take for granted. In these parts even the community nurses and child care nurses are shuttled around on the Flying Doctor Service's regular flights.

Landing on some of the strips can be a bit different from landing at Heathrow or JFK. First you 'buzz' the homestead so they know you have arrived, then you head for the strip – which could be five miles away. Next you buzz the strip to clear the livestock off. Then comes the tricky bit of actually landing.

Movies don't highlight the 20 minutes the medicos sit in the oppressive heat amidst dust and flies, wondering if anyone is on the way out to the strip to pick them up.

Hygiene

Aussies don't perspire or have a gentle glow, they sweat. By the end of a hot day they stink. Everyone showers every day and some even more often. The English can expect plenty of barbed comments on this subject because Aussies know for a fact they only wash once a week.

Bathtubs are a rare item but they are sometimes kept in older homes to remind the occupants of the earlier days of colonial rule. Modern houses have large recesses at the foot of their showers which may be referred to as baths, but their only practical use is for drowning the kids. There is no way an adult can actually stretch out in them.

In the Bathroom

Open an Aussie medicine cabinet and the outdoor life-style springs out at you: sunburn prevention creams everywhere and at least three different degrees of sun block, each in 57 different shades of luminous colours.

Plus sunburn treatment cream for the times when prevention didn't work.

The Aussies have the highest incidence of skin cancer in the world. Their sun is far more intense. The closer you are to the Equator the more acute the angle of the sun. It is useful to remember that it is ultra violet rays, not actual sunlight, that burn your skin – and these rays are not stopped by clouds. In the height of summer Aussies cover up even on overcast days.

It is little surprise that they take sunburn so seriously. Once burnt it will take a minimum of five years for the cancer to emerge.

Next come the sticking plasters in massive quantities which are a fair reflection of the fact that many playing areas are native bush. If the kids don't come in with at least one major cut a day they can't be getting enough exercise.

Then there is the assortment of calamine and insect bite lotions. What else for a country which has more things that bite than you could poke a stick at. And a lot more which will bite if you do.

Around the Kitchen

When it comes to the care of food the Aussies have learned to ignore every bit of European tradition. A few days in a kitchen and you will fully realize how far from home you are.

The refrigerators are not as big as they are just to hold the beer. Practically all the fruit and veggies find their way in. Obviously the heat in summer will ruin most things, yet this is only part of the problem. Wildlife is not restricted to the great outdoors. During daylight hours the flies make regular calls to every object in the kitchen.

The blowies (blowflies) are a daytime nightmare. Leave a piece of meat, a sausage, a pie or anything uncovered for a minute and it will be blown. You can't see the maggots for a while because they are too small, but they're there. Give it a few hours, and the food will get up and crawl out of the door.

Come evening and the enemy changes. Every house has cockroaches, earwigs, spiders and hundreds of other bugs lurking in dark places, waiting to crawl over every morsel of food in the house. If it got left out overnight it gets thrown out in the morning.

The Unexpected

In Australia it is not always what you expect that is hazardous to your health. Take bungarras. These are a variety of lizard which live in the sandy and desolate areas. They can grow to about six feet in length. Another name for them is 'race horse goannas' which should give some idea of how fast they move. Great tucker too, according to the Aborigines.

Bungarras have a very predictable reaction when they are startled. They run straight up the nearest tall object using their razor-sharp claws like talons for grip.

Of course if there are no trees, anybody standing near-by is going to end up with a new hat. The moment one of these lizards is startled in treeless country you can pick out the old bushies; they're the first to throw themselves flat on the ground.

Conversation and Gestures

If you want to know something, ask. The Aussies are not shy. They will soon tell you to "mind your own bloody business" if that's the way they feel.

There are no taboo conversations as such in Australia. None of this 'don't mention the war' stuff. Religion and politics are always good for an argument, so these are ideal conversation starters. But there are two topics that only fools would tackle with complete strangers: how much money a person earns, and race relations.

A discussion on race matters will achieve nothing positive. On the other hand it could reveal that your companion holds the common view that Aborigines are "unreliable, drunken bums" and that their drinking and voting rights should be taken back – prejudice that does little to help them, or your opinion of them.

It was the English settlers who plonked themselves down on a piece of the country and, looking only to the European countries for agreement, announced that they now owned the lot. This contempt set in train a way of thinking which has still not completely disappeared.

Weather

This is the universal topic, but care should be taken not to get too generalised with your remarks. The country is 2,000 miles from north to south – that's about the same distance as from Norway to the south of Spain.

Australia may be the flattest continent in the world and also one of the hottest, but these are just statistics; reality is a lot different. Tasmania, for instance, hardly has any flat ground and when it's not cold and wet, it is just plain cold. It rains there for six months of the year and the water drips off the trees for the other six months.

Aussies have more snow than the Swiss. It doesn't fall in many places, but the size of the area in which it does fall is larger than Switzerland.

A huge mountain range stretches almost the entire length of the East coast. For most of its length it is called the Great Dividing Range – i.e. inland it's dry, and on the coastal strip it's wet and fertile.

More than half the East coast, over a thousand miles, gets more than 75 inches of rain each year. Some towns in the far north of Queensland get around 250 inches (about the height of a double-decker bus).

When inland areas don't get rain every year they get 'a bit warm'. The locals would not use the term 'hot' if it's only around 'a century' because they would have nothing left to describe a day of 140°F in polite company.

Hot and dry is nowhere near as bad as hot and humid. Try sleeping some night when it is still over 90°F at midnight and the air is as sticky as a sauna. This is not the outback either, this is Brisbane, Sydney and Perth in late summer. (In fact it's Brisbane for all of the summer.)

Eighty-five per cent of the population live in the quite temperate coastal regions and this is where all the state capitals are located. In the capitals a summer temperature of a century will rate a particular note in the weather reports. Successive daily centuries can add a bit of sadistic interest to some otherwise miserable days.

In winter, after listing the known state centres in which rain is forecast, the weather men announce that it will be fine 'elsewhere'. There are many winter days when that is exactly where a lot of people would rather be.

Insults

Insult the Aussies at your own peril. Although they are slow to anger they are much slower to forget. Forgiveness is a totally foreign concept.

If you really feel you must insult an Aussie male try calling him a 'pooftah'. It's not so much the inference of homosexuality that drives the dagger in – it's the inference that he is not exactly what he appears to be.

Gestures are all the normal ones. Nobody is going to split hairs over whether you should use one or two fingers, just so long as your palm is facing inwards. These gestures are used extensively between motorists.

The most ominous gesture you could get from an Aussie is a smile.

Custom and Tradition

The most widely held Australian tradition is a once-a-year bet on the horses. On the first Tuesday in November the entire country comes to a standstill as the Melbourne Cup is run. The Victorians even get paid time off work to attend.

There is no explanation for the Aussies' obsession with this race. The remainder of the year the sport of kings has much less appeal but for this one race an average of six dollars is bet for every man, woman and child in the country.

In a land so different and with such unusual people you could hardly expect the customs and traditions all to have a familiar flavour. Traditions are not much steeped in time and many have a strong flavour of participation.

Simplicity is always a big factor.

State Rivalry

With the country so isolated from the rest of the world it would be easy to assume that a feeling of unity would arise. This is a long way from the truth when you look at relationships between the states. The states of Australia are politically more independent of each other than are the countries of the United Kingdom. The common bond of insanity can become quite regionalised.

Name calling is the customary Australian way to react in these situations. The less populated states have the most distinct traditions in this regard and, no matter how derogatory, each of them wears theirs with pride.

South Australians are called 'crow eaters'. No doubt from some early reflection on the poor farming quality of much of the northern part of that state. The place is so desolate and dusty that their crows have to fly backwards to keep the dust out of their eyes.

Only the Western Australians could accept the title of 'sandgropers' so easily. They have even invented a stuffed toy sandgroper to cash in on their name. (It is sold to raise funds for charity.) There are plenty of advantages in living in a border to border sand pit but an abundance of water is not one of them.

The other states have names that tend to change from time to time. People from New South Wales could be called 'magpies'. The magpies will call the Victorians 'Mexicans' – because they're south of the border.

Queensland is the one state that really is different from all the others. It has rain forests, lush coastal strips, the Great Barrier Reef and bananas. There is no disputing that Queenslanders are the most peculiar people. Australia's early European ancestry is alive and well amongst the 'banana benders'.

Anzac Day

The Aussies are reverent once a year. On 25th April, old soldiers get their uniforms out and march proudly down the main street of every town right across the country.

The loss of Aussie lives by war has been horrendous. Seen in terms of numbers internationally they may seem insignificant but as a proportion of the male youth of a young and growing country the losses were catastrophic.

There are only three times a year that Aussie pubs are barred from opening (though this is slowly being relaxed). They are Christmas day, New Year's day and the morning of Anzac day. These three days are also the only public holidays which fall on the same day each year.

In the morning the men march and remember the dead. In the afternoon they drink.

Cake Stalls

The custom of holding cake stalls is one fund-raising practice that must never be allowed to disappear. In the smaller rural communities there is too much pride for local organizations to beg their neighbours for money. This is not the Aussie way. They will raise money by selling home-made products from a trestle in the street.

If you are a lover of real jam and real cakes you must buy from a cake stall, particularly if it is being run by the Country Women's Association. The highest standard of goods is absolutely guaranteed. Every contribution for sale is thoroughly scrutinised – by all the neighbours or at least a committee of gossipers which ensures the same effect. Being found guilty of contributing runny jam or of baking a packet cake is a public humiliation from which there is no reprieve.

The Family Picnic

A traditional Aussie picnic is not to be missed. This is not a pleasant drive down a leafy country lane with lunch on a grassy hillside. This is survival in the wild.

These mandatory forms of punishment are carried out in the native bush, sometimes near water and always well out of the city boundaries. This is obviously in answer to some hereditary urge to recreate the hardships of the early settlers. The ridiculous thing is that the settlers only ate in the bush because they had no other choice.

You could conjure up a dismal scene based only on the heat, dust, rocky ground and every imaginable variety of rough and prickly shrub. But add the wildlife and you have an unforgettable combination.

If it creeps, crawls, wriggles, slithers, walks, runs, jumps, flies, flutters or glides, it lives in Australia. And you will probably meet it on the picnic, right when you least expect it.

This is a country full of venomous snakes and spiders, some of them particularly vicious, but the Aussies will wander around the bush with little apparent regard for things that could kill or maim them and encourage you to do the same.

What you are not being told is that because they've been exposed to the bush since birth, their avoidance of obvious danger spots is instinctive. You are not so lucky. Some of the ants alone are one inch long and if you sit in the wrong spot you will remember them for many painful hours.

The first order of the picnic is to get the fire going. Scoop out a bit of ground and form a circle of rocks. Not bad. So far you have found two centipedes, a scorpion, a red back spider (venomous), several ant colonies and heard 'something' rustle off into the scrub. Now you have to wander through acres of bush, tearing limbs and clothing to gather the firewood.

Dispel any romantic thoughts you have of a genuine Aussie bush barbecue – settle for the domesticated version every time.

One way or another a piece of tin is suspended above the fire and the sausages are thrown on first. The sausages ooze the fat for the steaks to come, and because they're quick to cook, you can get the kids out of your hair much sooner. How do you like your steak – well done, burnt, or charcoal? And is that with or without the sand?

You can't sit down and eat because of the crawling insects. Standing up eating and swatting flies is a memory you will take with you for ever.

Hatched, Matched and Despatched

The Aussies are such an easy-going mob of individuals that they will tolerate just about anything. With such mixed ethnic backgrounds they have had to. Every European nationality is represented and as a result the treatment of birth, death, marriage and divorce is different in every family.

Religion is not strong, but if you've got it, that's fine – what are you doing *after* church on Sunday? The advantage is with the non-religious; they get a couple of extra hours' recreation per week.

More than one third of Australian marriages end in divorce, so in many cases it hardly seems worth wasting a perfectly good Saturday afternoon on a wedding. But marriage is tolerated and, if there are to be kids from the union, it is even quite common.

At funerals nobody will interfere. If you want to wail, cry or scream, go right ahead. The worst that would be said of you is you "must be one of the weirder nationalities".

47

Crime and Punishment

Crime can be a bit mystifying to the Aussies. They get caught between a complete disregard for rules and authority and their trust in people's sense of fair play.

But within this framework a criminal can have honour and respect. It's deceit that offends the trust; if a crook is honest and does not commit a crime against normal people, no harm is done.

Crime, to be acceptable, must contain itself within the bounds of fair play. An offence against a weaker opponent is heinous. Don't even think of mugging the young or elderly. Someone slightly bigger and aware of the risks is fair game. He ought to have known better.

Everyday criminal and traffic laws are enacted by each state individually. The laws are therefore not uniform and neither are the punishments. Laws relating to corporate offences are enacted in each state but in a rare act of co-operation these are done uniformly.

Offences against the federal Income Tax Act are hardly regarded as crimes. The bolder the tax offender, the higher the hero status. Tax laws are fair game. It is a national preoccupation to beat the tax office. This offends no Aussie principles – the tax office is well staffed with competent people. As tax is the nearest thing to the blood of government there is much satisfaction in seeing it spilt.

In the same spirit it is not regarded as an offence to break the traffic laws. It is only an offence to get caught doing so. It is elevated to being a crime only if that offence ends in harm to somebody.

One of Australia's most notable national folk heroes is Ned Kelly, a bushranger from the last part of the 19th century. Ned Kelly and his gang are regarded with respect for supposed acts of daring and courage in stealing. It is a term of praise to be described 'as game as Ned Kelly'.

One of the lowest incidences of sex crimes is in Kalgoorlie in the Western Australian goldfields. This is despite a very low proportion of women in this isolated centre of the mining region.

Locals will proudly explain that Kalgoorlie's luck in this regard is attributable to the 'knocker shops' – brothels which lie together on Hay Street, along with the police station, court house, church, school, hospital, commercial sites and private houses.

Take a drive down Hay Street on a pay night (every second Thursday) and you will see long lines of men lined up and chatting pleasantly while they wait their turn outside their favourite woman's door.

Police in Australia are generally tolerant and don't make too much nuisance of themselves. They're in fact very helpful and patient. If you are lost or need help ask the nearest police constable.

Australian police are halfway between their American and English counterparts. That is, about half the police carry side arms. (It's a matter of personal choice.)

Firearms are not freely available to the public although rural landholders can get a rifle licence for pest control (shooting kangaroos, rabbits and foxes). Handguns for shooting your spouse or neighbours are illegal – as indeed would be the actual shooting.

There are many offences, particularly related to such dreadful deeds as appearing drunk in a public place, which can land you in a lock-up overnight. This is not a pleasant experience as sleep is not permitted to be uninterrupted, the porridge is revolting and the toast is always served cold.

It is in the jail system that the classification of crimes is made clear. At one end of the scale the white collar criminals, who commit fraud and embezzlement, go to low security prison farms which have nothing more than stock fences to keep them in. Their crimes are hardly very serious if they were only committed on paper.

At the other end of the scale the violent sex offenders and serial murderers will get solitary confinement in maximum security. The solitary is for their own protection from the other inmates who, as society's representatives, would exact vengeance.

If Robin Hood were alive today he'd be an Aussie.

Systems

Despite their obvious preference for an unsophisticated image, the Aussies run their public services on a fairly hi-tech basis. They also have the advantage of having had their infrastructures developed in modern times and with some degree of forward planning.

But they also have one severe disadvantage. They are an expanding country and development is always three paces behind need. Don't whinge to the Aussies if something is not quite right – they're probably not too happy about it either.

Public Transport

If you get a bus to within a mile of a suburban destination within an hour of the time you want, you can count yourself lucky. It's not that the bus is late, erratic or lost, there just aren't that many.

Buses, trains and trams service city centres well. There is constant promotional effort by the cities to get people out of their cars and on to public transport. This, however, is not the Australian way.

Every Aussie, from the age of 17 upwards, can drive. It would be impossible to survive in either the suburbs or the bush without a vehicle.

Buses are used the most for moving long distances on the ground. One notable exception is the Indian Pacific Railway which covers the two and a half thousand miles from Sydney to Perth in three days.

When it comes to planes you can get a scheduled flight almost anywhere. This is the only practical way to cover some of these distances and landscapes. It is also a great way to miss out on seeing some unique sights.

Roads

Look out for yourself on the road because nobody else will. Everybody knows the rules and it is assumed that they will be obeyed. None of this polite 'after you' stuff. If an Aussie has the right of way, and this will be very obvious from one of the hundred signs on each intersection, slam on your brakes.

For all minor offences the police are able to issue on-the-spot fines. If you don't pay this fine the charge will go to court, with or without you, and the costs will increase dramatically. The Aussie approach is to try like hell to talk their way out of the ticket in the first place.

The car culture breeds car parks. Acres and acres of them. By the time you have found a park in a suburban shopping centre on a Saturday morning you are half a mile from the entrance.

It is little consolation that the centre is air-conditioned. On a hot summer's day nothing can compensate for that walk around the sea of cars looking for yours. When you do get there, you open the door only to collapse into something akin to a furnace.

Roobars

On the front of many vehicles in the back of beyond is a set of steel bars. The main purpose of these bars is to hold the roos off when you meet them unexpectedly on a dark road.

Roobars work pretty well for small roos, for saplings you hit when you run off the road, for bluffing city traffic into giving way and for getting pedestrians to back up. But for the big roo who is stupid enough to stop, mid hop, in front of a car doing 80 miles an hour, no bar is going to help. The bar itself will end up in the cabin.

Roos can be a real nuisance on the roads. Their best trick is to jump just before they get hit. Straight through the windscreen and you have one upset kangaroo thrashing around the interior with some dangerous hind legs. This is no problem to any cool driver though, he's got the motor off, the hand brake on, and is already halfway out of the door long before the car stops.

Sleek, sharp-nosed sports cars are a laugh when they meet a kangaroo. The front, instead of bashing the roo down, scoops it up and straight along the bonnet. So much for the windscreen and roof (and anybody's head that gets in the way).

Road Trains

In the flat outback regions the Aussies have come up with a cross between a truck and a train. A prime mover and trailer (around 35 feet long and probably loaded with cattle) will have a 'dog' (another trailer) hitched on. In fact it could have half a dozen dogs.

These are dangerous things to try and overtake if you ever manage to catch up to one. The dust and rocks being thrown up mix wonderfully with the constant shower of cow piss. If you don't have nerves of steel, a full bottle of windscreen washing water and a laminated windscreen you don't attempt to pass.

One story doing the rounds, tells of a public-spirited road-train driver who gave a tow to a couple of women who had got themselves stranded miles from anywhere. From the moment he got moving they tried flashing their lights and blowing their horn to get him to stop, but he was oblivious to their plight and in all probability had completely forgotten about them.

When he did stop about an hour down the road the women were cowering on the floor of the car. There were no lights left, no windscreen and very little paint on any forward-facing surface.

Fire Brigade

In such a large dry country the rural fire brigades are a serious matter. Contributions towards their cost of maintenance are compulsory for land owners. In the event of a fire everyone participates.

In the rural communities neighbours are not admired for their daring in flaunting fire regulations. Once a fire gets going it is not likely to be restricted to one farm.

In the station country (outback) the distances are so vast and resources so scarce that bush fires are left to burn themselves out. The fire could easily travel hundreds of miles over several weeks before it runs out of steam (so to speak).

Farmers in the closer communities don't wait to be called to a fire. If they see smoke they will get their fire-fighting rig on to the tractor and head towards it. After a fire is controlled the immediate neighbours will continue to encircle the 'burn', guarding their own paddocks, until the last ember has died.

However, the Aussies' inherently casual attitude to disaster is never far away. A few years ago, in a tiny wheatbelt town on a very cold winter's night, a small wooden house caught fire. The three occupants were itinerant farm workers and down at the pub at the time.

The sole effect of the fire truck tearing through the township was to draw the whole population to the fire. Nobody lifted a finger towards putting out the flames. This was the greatest entertainment and warmest social gathering for weeks. The party didn't break up until the house was no more.

Schooling and Qualifications

Schooling in Australia is relatively uniform. At primary and secondary level the only difference between someone who attended a private school and someone who attended government school is the income of the parents. At tertiary level there is not even that difference.

The old school tie is therefore of little value once you are in the job market.

The value of qualifications varies according to the trade. Basically they are useful in getting the first interview; from then on, you're on your own. The fact that qualifications are handed out by governments and institutions is not lost on employers.

Australia's school year begins and ends with the calendar year and all children start school at about the age of six. However, an absurd situation is caused by lack of uniformity between the states. There is not enough co-operation to overcome the differences in the exact starting age.

In one state children might start in the first year in which they are five on the first day of school, in another it could be the year in which they are six by the end of the school year, and in yet another it will be the year during which they have their sixth birthday.

Changing residences between states with school-aged children born either very early or very late in the year turns into a nightmare as you argue to maintain their position.

Government and Bureaucracy

When Australia was settled by the British, the colony was controlled from the other side of the world. Since that time Australia has undergone several dramatic spurts of growth – the latest being immediately after the Second World War when large-scale immigration was encouraged.

The sheer demand created by these events meant that no government could possibly keep up with the need for facilities and regulations. Government has been a constant restraint on the development of the country. Restraint is appreciated by nobody, but to the energetic Aussies it is unforgivable. Breaking a government regulation is not a crime, it is an act of revenge.

Australia is still a member of the Commonwealth and as such is subject to the control of Governors appointed by the Queen. This situation was brought dramatically into focus in 1974 when the Governor General (an Aussie now living in exile in England) sacked the Labor government and appointed the Opposition Party as caretakers until a new election could be held.

Many modern Australians have no historic links with

the United Kingdom and the move to republicanism is fast gaining ground. The fact that the Aussie Queen is also the Queen of England is not seen as a particular problem; everybody has a right to hold a second job. But that she is a Pom and lives in England really brings her relevance to the Aussies into question.

Australia has three tiers of government:

- federal
- state
- local.

Each level is contested by two major political parties – although less strongly at the local level. The more left of the two is the Labor Party and the less left is the Liberal Party. They also have the usual collection of the radical lefts, the radical rights and the just plain radical.

Federal Government

The Federation of the States of Australia came about on the first day of this century.

The Federal Parliament was originally located in Melbourne but this was found to be too close to real people. In 1910 an area about the size of Luxembourg was annexed from the south of New South Wales and became the Australian Capital Territory. Federal Government is now safely closeted there, in Canberra, out of everybody's way.

The main differences from the English system, on which it is styled, is that the members of the Upper House are Senators not Lords, the language used is far more colourful and the abuse far more personal.

The Federal Government is held directly responsible for defence against any misguided invaders, the loss of any international game of sport, and all the economic ills of every family in the country.

State Governments

Each of the States also has two independently elected Houses of Parliament. Pity the residents of any state ruled by the opposite party to the one which is in power in Canberra.

The Australian Constitution says there can be no restriction on trade between the states but the State Governments mount enormous campaigns to discourage such trade by inciting parochial pride.

The State Governments are held directly responsible for the loss of any interstate game of sport, or if a child ends up illiterate, or if your mate gets picked up for drunk driving, or if the train is late, or if the weather is lousy on the day of the family picnic.

Local Government

Each State is divided into municipalities which have their own elected council. Aspiring politicians vent their early enthusiasm on these councils. Also usually well represented are the property developers and real estate firms.

The local councils are held directly responsible for any storms which fell the trees over roads, for lack of a local doctor, for approving your neighbour's land re-zoning and for refusing you permission to build a tanning factory in the middle of the township.

Business

The Australian business scene is in a constant state of change. Population growth and mobility present many opportunities to challenge the existing players.

Good Aussies never refuse a challenge. Once they have a house and their family under way there is only one serious challenge left – to beat the big boys at their own game.

Full time employment is something they put up with while waiting for the right chance to present itself. The security of employment is nothing compared with the thrill of possible financial ruin. Employers live with the fact that their best workers are only biding their time, waiting for an opportunity to set up against them.

Despite this quite competitive streak, fair play is never too far beneath the surface. A person's pride is worth more than a couple of extra dollars. Naturally the situation could be different if we are talking about more than a couple of dollars.

Company Hierarchy

The best person for the job is always overlooked when promotion comes along. All Aussies know that the good guys never win. They know that even if a 'decent' person does get a promotion their character changes as soon as they get a bit of power.

It is therefore obvious that all bosses are fools and not worthy of respect. This is the starting point for anyone of a higher rank. Formality and blind following of traditions are as absent from business life as they are in any other part of Aussie life. In business familiarity does not breed contempt, it breeds respect. Juniors refer to their seniors as Mr or Mrs only against the threat of the sack. The company manager who does not know the first name of every junior commands no respect.

The Independent Business

Almost the entire house building industry is conducted by self-employed contractors. This has forced the governments and trade associations to introduce tight regulations to protect hapless home-owners from the Ned Kellys of the industry. (Innovation is the polite term for the short cuts they often take in order to get the job done in the shortest time possible.)

If an unlicensed person so much as touches an electric power point the householder's insurance could be invalidated.

The high street shops and suburban stores are continually changing owners as people 'give it a go' for a while. The general pattern is to work like hell in a seven-day-a-week corner store for about three years then sell the business and have six months off. Practically every newsagency in Australia is owned by a retired bank manager.

The published failure rates amongst small business operators are alarmingly high but this is caused by two main factors. The first is that statistics are deliberately compiled in such a way as to present an alarming picture. This is a vain attempt to force people to think more carefully before following along like a mob of sheep.

The second cause is purely the Aussie nature. They are so determined to set up on their own that they will take any risk at all. It's a heck of a lot more fun than being safe.

Culture

Development of land and communities in Australia had a much higher priority than development of the arts. So if you are not a great lover of the cultured things in life you can relax in Australia – you will have nothing thrust upon you. If you are, you will have to search it out.

The centrepiece of Australian culture is the Sydney Opera House – once described as 'a huddle of nuns in a high wind'. It might be part of the national pride now, but it certainly wasn't during construction. It had enormous overruns of both time and cost and was loudly proclaimed a white elephant. Much of the funding came from huge national lotteries which were enthusiastically supported by the Aussies. Just by buying a ticket you could claim to be 'a supporter of the arts'.

There are many examples of imported culture but if it's purely Aussie culture you are seeking then there is a barb of truth in the saying: 'There is more culture in a small tub of yogurt than there is in the whole of Australia.'

If there is one name that strikes a chord with Aussies it is that of Banjo Paterson, the person responsible for *Waltzing Matilda*.

He first came to light in 1880 when the *Sydney Bulletin* decided to encourage bushmen (real and imaginary ones) to contribute verse and stories of life in the outback. The portrayal of life which surfaced through the paper has endowed the country with a recorded history so colourful as to more than make up for its lack of years.

The most famous pair of writers from this period were Banjo Paterson and Henry Lawson, who shared a mutual disregard for each other's views. This friction eventually erupted into the 'War of the Bards' which raged on and on through the pages of the newspaper.

In one of Banjo Paterson's many poems *The Travelling*

Post Office there is disturbing evidence of real literary talent. It is the story of a letter posted to a drover 'Care of Conroy's sheep'. The first verse goes like this:

> The roving breezes come and go, the reed beds sweep and
> sway,
> The sleepy river murmurs low, and loiters on its way.
> It is the land of lots o'time along the Castlereagh.

And later:

> The sheep are travelling for the grass, and travelling very
> slow;
> They may be at Mundooran now, or past the Overflow,
> Or tramping down the black soil flats across by Waddiwong,
> But all those little country towns would send the letter wrong,
> The mailman, if he's extra tired, would pass them in his
> sleep,
> It's safest to address the note to 'Care of Conroy's sheep'.
> For five and twenty thousand head can scarcely go astray,
> You write to 'Care of Conroy's sheep along the Castlereagh'.

And ends:

> Beneath a sky of deepest blue where never cloud abides,
> A speck upon the waste of plain the lonely mailman rides.
> Where fierce hot winds have set the pine and myall boughs
> asweep
> He hails the shearers passing by for news of Conroy's sheep.
> By big lagoons where wildfowl play and crested pigeons
> flock,
> By campfires where the drovers ride around their restless
> stock,
> And past the teamster toiling down to fetch the wool away
> My letter chases Conroy's sheep along the Castlereagh.

Language and Ideas

The entire Australian population would be remarkable if they were judged on their linguistic skills alone. Yet this characteristic is not often identified.

All Aussies possess the mental dexterity to write fluently in one language (basically English with a few Americanisms thrown in) and yet speak an entirely different language.

It is when it comes to the spoken one that you will realize you are amongst foreigners. This is the language increasingly referred to as 'Strine', one that enhances English with a colour and vigour to suit the Aussie character. Just the act of reserving Strine for conversation frees it from the risk of restrictive definitions.

The purpose of conversation is clearly to convey information. No Aussie is going to see it as anything more. It is neither an art form nor an inheritance from some classic literary past. Words can get joined together, abbreviated and even missed out, so learning it is out of the question. It is a matter of listening carefully. A 'coupla' samples are:

driza – it is as dry as a
jawanna – do you want a

With rhyming slang getting mixed in there as well, you will get some incomprehensible local words. On one particular surfing beach three new words were created to describe surfers from outside the district:

euros – Europeans
touros – Australians
seppos – Americans

(Americans are yanks. Yanks rhymes with tanks. The worst kind of tanks are septic tanks and seppos is short for septic tanks. It's all so logical.)

Most bastards reckon that the Aussies use swear words in every bloody sentence the buggers ever utter. This is not new. One shocked English visitor more than a hundred years ago recorded: 'Your thoroughbred gumsucker never speaks without apostrophising his oath and interlarding his diction with the crimsonest of adjectives.'

The Aussies are not subtle and neither is their language. They will say what they mean. The problem is that the words they use don't always mean what they say. For example:

bluey – someone who has red hair
you're orright – you are absolutely super
itsa bit warm – it is probably 120°F in the water bag
    (water bags are always hung in the shade)
that'd be right – I don't believe it either.

Another Aussie rule is: why use conventional descriptive phrases when there is a humorous one that will do? This produces some colourful results, such as:

flat out like a lizard drinking – doing nothing
off like a bucket of prawns in the sun – moved like
    lightning
drier than a dead dingo's donger – very thirsty
wouldn't shout if a shark bit him – won't buy a beer

The key to picking up the meaning of Strine is to watch the faces of those who are speaking. If they are not scowling it is probable that what sounds like an insult is in fact a compliment. This is not completely reliable though; you have to remember that they are a far from homogeneous group of people.

The Aussies through their language demonstrate their individuality, their vigorous character, their lack of convention and their directness. It's been said before and it's worth saying again – they're a weird mob.

The Author

The author is named Joseph Kenneth Hunt, but he is called 'Ken'. Until he was 14 years old he believed his name was Kenneth Joe Hunt. All his school records are in that name. But needing his birth certificate for something or other, the truth was revealed.

According to his mother he was called Ken after his uncle, and because his father is called Joe. Had he been called Joe, he'd have been nicknamed 'Little Joey' (which is a baby roo).

In fact it turns out that his father's name is not Joe, it's Percy – Percy Joseph Kelly Hunt. He was called Joe because his real name would also have made his younger days intolerable. Joe's father died when he was about two. When he was 21 he changed his name to Hunt after his stepfather, but retained the name Kelly. He thought of hyphenating it to Kelly-Hunt but that would have made his later life intolerable.

It further transpires that Kelly is not the family name. Joe's father was press-ganged by the Royal Navy, jumped ship in Portsmouth and assumed the name Kelly.

Proof of Ken's lack of concern over this confusion has resulted in his daughter being named Jo.

During his life Ken has managed a dodgem track, picked fruit, been a messenger boy, painter, accountant, business consultant and owned a general store. In Australia he has lived in three states and eight towns and cities. He has travelled widely in Europe, Canada, America, China, Russia, Asia and big-time islands like Jersey, Guernsey, the Isle of Man, Grand Cayman and the Bahamas.

He claims the fact that the latter are all tax havens has made no difference whatsoever to his appreciation of them.